C000229697

USA Patriot Act: Better Interagency
Coordination and Implementing Guidance
for Section 311 Could Improve U.S. Anti-
Money Laundering Efforts: GAO-08-1058

U.S. Government Accountability Office (GAO)

The BiblioGov Project is an effort to expand awareness of the public documents and records of the U.S. Government via print publications. In broadening the public understanding of government and its work, an enlightened democracy can grow and prosper. Ranging from historic Congressional Bills to the most recent Budget of the United States Government, the BiblioGov Project spans a wealth of government information. These works are now made available through an environmentally friendly, print-on-demand basis, using only what is necessary to meet the required demands of an interested public. We invite you to learn of the records of the U.S. Government, heightening the knowledge and debate that can lead from such publications.

Included are the following Collections:

Budget of The United States Government
Presidential Documents
United States Code
Education Reports from ERIC
GAO Reports
History of Bills
House Rules and Manual
Public and Private Laws

Code of Federal Regulations
Congressional Documents
Economic Indicators
Federal Register
Government Manuals
House Journal
Privacy act Issuances
Statutes at Large

United States Government Accountability Office

GAO

Report to Congressional Requesters

September 2008

USA PATRIOT ACT

Better Interagency Coordination and Implementing Guidance for Section 311 Could Improve U.S. Anti-Money Laundering Efforts

GAO

Accountability ★ Integrity ★ Reliability

GAO-08-1058

September 2008

Highlights

Highlights of GAO-08-1058, a report to congressional requesters

USA PATRIOT ACT

Better Interagency Coordination and Implementing Guidance for Section 311 Could Improve U.S. Anti-Money Laundering Efforts

Why GAO Did This Study

Since September 11, 2001, the United States has established tools to address the threat to the U.S. financial system of money laundering and terrorist financing. One such tool is Section 311 of the USA PATRIOT Act of 2001, which authorizes the Secretary of the Treasury (Treasury) to prohibit U.S. financial institutions from maintaining certain accounts for foreign banks if they involve foreign jurisdictions or institutions found to be of primary money laundering concern. To make this finding, Treasury examines several factors and generally issues a proposed rule announcing its intent to apply Section 311 restrictions.

GAO was asked to examine (1) the process used to implement Section 311 restrictions, (2) the process Treasury follows to finalize or withdraw a proposed rule, and (3) how Treasury assesses the impact of Section 311.

GAO reviewed financial and investigative U.S. government documents and met with government officials and representatives of affected banks

What GAO Recommends

GAO recommends that Treasury establish guidance to clarify responsibility to implement and finalize Section 311 actions.

Treasury said it will act in response to this recommendation, although the process has been improved. Justice and State did not comment.

To view the full product, including the scope and methodology, click on GAO-08-1058. For more information, contact Loren Yager at (202) 512-4347 or yagerl@gao.gov.

What GAO Found

Treasury's informal process to implement Section 311 was consistent with requirements in U.S. law. From 2002 to 2005, Treasury identified 11 cases--3 jurisdictions and 8 institutions--as being of primary money laundering concern and issued proposed rules for 10 of these cases. As required, Treasury consulted with the Departments of Justice and State prior to issuing the proposed rules. However, Justice and State officials said that it was difficult for them to effectively assess the evidence on some Section 311 cases because Treasury provided them limited time. In 2006, Treasury changed its process by forming an interagency working group to discuss potential threats to the U.S. financial system. But it is unclear if the new process addressed the agencies' concerns since Treasury has issued no Section 311 findings since 2005.

Treasury determines whether to finalize or withdraw a proposed Section 311 rule by reviewing written comments and sometimes meeting with interested parties. The duration of a proposed rule is significant because U.S. financial institutions act immediately in response to its announcement. However, Treasury has taken years to complete this process in some cases. In April 2008, Treasury withdrew two of three notices--all open for between 3 and 5 years--after GAO discussed the cases with Treasury officials. Contributing to this lag was the absence of required timeframes for completing the action and of written guidance specifying a Treasury office to finalize the actions.

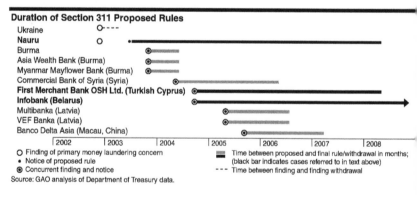

Duration of Section 311 Proposed Rules

| | 2002 | 2003 | 2004 | 2005 | 2006 | 2007 | 2008 |

○ Finding of primary money laundering concern
• Notice of proposed rule
◎ Concurrent finding and notice
▬▬ Time between proposed and final rule/withdrawal in months; (black bar indicates cases referred to in text above)
- - - Time between finding and finding withdrawal
Source: GAO analysis of Department of Treasury data.

Treasury views Section 311 as effective because it isolates target institutions from the U.S. financial system and encourages some foreign governments to strengthen their anti-money laundering authorities. However, some foreign government officials said that Section 311's implementation precluded their own enforcement or regulatory actions against targeted institutions as U.S. action was unilateral or provided too little information for them to act. Justice officials said that if Section 311's application is viewed as unsubstantiated, some countries may be less likely to cooperate with the U.S. government on other law enforcement matters or sanctions. Treasury officials recognized the concerns, but did not believe they diminished Section 311's effectiveness.

Contents

Tables

Figures

Abbreviations

AFMLS	Asset Forfeiture & Money Laundering Section
BSA	Bank Secrecy Act
FATF	Financial Action Task Force
FBI	Federal Bureau of Investigation
FinCEN	Financial Crimes Enforcement Network
NCCT	Non-Cooperative Countries and Territories
OFAC	Office of Foreign Assets Control
TFFC	Terrorist Financing and Financial Crimes
TFI	Office of Terrorism and Financial Intelligence
USA PATRIOT	Uniting and Protecting America by Providing Appropriate Tools Required to Intercept and Obstruct Terrorism

United States Government Accountability Office
Washington, DC 20548

September 30, 2008

Congressional Requesters

Countries with lax anti-money laundering regulation and enforcement pose a national security threat to the United States because they provide financial safe havens for criminal enterprise.[1] Money laundering—the process of disguising or concealing illicit funds to make them appear legitimate—is an increasingly serious issue, with new payment and communications technologies opening up the world to transnational crime and creating new options for cross-border funds transfers. Since September 11, 2001, the United States has established a number of tools to address the threat of money laundering and terrorist financing to the U.S. financial system. One of its new tools was enacted in Section 311 of the Uniting and Strengthening America by Providing Appropriate Tools Required to Intercept and Obstruct Terrorism (USA PATRIOT) Act of 2001.[2] The goals of Section 311 include strengthening U.S. measures to prevent, detect, and prosecute international money laundering and the financing of terrorism. In particular, Section 311 provides a mechanism for the U.S. government either to prohibit U.S. financial institutions from maintaining correspondent accounts[3] with a foreign financial institution if the account involves jurisdictions or institutions found to be of primary money laundering concern, or to require recordkeeping and reporting on certain accounts. The Department of the Treasury (Treasury) has implemented the Section 311 mechanism against eight targeted financial institutions and three jurisdictions in eight countries since 2002. Under the law, this mechanism was imposed in most cases by rule-making–including notice of the proposed rule and a comment period before the rule is finalized. However, particular applications of Section 311 restrictions raised questions in Congress about how effectively Section 311 was being used.

---

[1]National Money Laundering Strategy for 2007 (U.S. Government, Washington, D.C.: 2007).

[2]Pub. L. 107-56, 115 Stat 272 (Oct. 26, 2001).

[3]A correspondent account is an account established by a banking institution to receive deposits from, make payments on behalf of, or handle other financial transactions for another financial institution.

GAO-08-1058 USA Patriot Act

In this report, we (1) examined the process U. S. agencies used to implement the USA PATRIOT Act Section 311 restrictions against targeted financial institutions and countries and the results of these actions; (2) assessed the process Treasury follows to determine whether to finalize or withdraw a proposed rule; and (3) described how Treasury assesses the impact of Section 311 restrictions.

To meet these objectives, we reviewed program documentation and interviewed knowledgeable officials from key U.S. agencies at the Department of Justice (Justice), Department of State (State), Treasury, and the Board of Governors of the Federal Reserve System (Federal Reserve) in Washington, D.C. We focused this performance audit on all locations where the U.S. government has targeted financial institutions or jurisdictions for Section 311 actions. These were Belarus, Burma, Latvia, Macau, Nauru, Syria, Turkish Republic of Northern Cyprus, and Ukraine. We met with U.S. and foreign government officials, and representatives of financial institutions and financial institution associations, and reviewed documents in Kyiv, Ukraine; Macau and Hong Kong, China; and Riga, Latvia. We visited Kyiv, Ukraine; Macau and Hong Kong, China; and Riga, Latvia, because they provided examples of different applications of Section 311, specifically a targeted jurisdiction and targeted financial institutions where Section 311 restrictions were finalized and withdrawn. Treasury provided us with key documents it identified to show how it implemented its 311 process. A detailed description of our scope and methodology is included in appendix I of this report. We conducted this performance audit from September 2007 through September 2008 in accordance with generally accepted government auditing standards. Those standards require that we plan and perform the audit to obtain sufficient, appropriate evidence to provide a reasonable basis for our findings and conclusions based on our audit objectives. We believe that the evidence obtained provides a reasonable basis for our findings and conclusions based on our audit objectives.

Results in Brief

To implement USA PATRIOT Act Section 311, Treasury used an evolving informal rule-making process that followed requirements set forth in U.S. law and modified this process after 2005.[4] However, while Treasury's

---

[4]Throughout this report, implementation refers to all aspects of the Section 311 process, including targeting, publishing findings of primary money laundering concern and notices of proposed rule making, and publishing final rules and withdrawals.

process from 2002 through 2005 considered statutory factors established in Section 311,[5] its process for consulting with two U.S. agencies on findings of primary money laundering concern sometimes made it difficult to provide meaningful consultation during certain key phases of the process, according to relevant agency officials. For the purpose of using the new Section 311 authority, Treasury independently developed a list of targeted financial institutions derived from several sources. It next researched evidence for each targeted institution on the list to consider factors established in Section 311. As a result, Treasury issued a finding in the *Federal Register* that each of the eight financial institutions[6] were of primary money laundering concern and a proposed rule announcing its intent to apply restrictions on the institutions. Before the proposed rule was issued for public comment, Treasury provided it to Justice and State, agencies with expertise in money laundering and international affairs, for consultation on the finding, as required by the act. However, in some cases, these agencies had limited time available to review documentary evidence—as little as 2 days—and in one case limited access to facilities for discussing classified information within the short time frames, according to Justice and State officials. In the absence of operational guidance with set time frames for this consultation requirement, officials of these agencies expressed concern over the amount of time and procedures they had for consultation. Starting in 2006, Treasury changed its targeting procedures and, with Justice, established an interagency working group to discuss potential threats to the U.S. financial system at an earlier stage in the process. However, it is unclear whether the new procedures improved this aspect of consultation because Treasury's current targeting process has not resulted in any new Section 311 findings since 2005.

Treasury determines whether to finalize or withdraw a proposed rule under Section 311 by reviewing written comments and other information it receives from interested parties in a process consistent with rule-making requirements in the Administrative Procedure Act. However, Treasury has taken years to complete this process for some cases, in part because (1)

---

[5]For example, one factor to consider is the substance and quality of the administration of the bank supervisory and counter-money laundering laws of the jurisdiction.

[6]In targeting the three jurisdictions—the countries of Burma, Nauru, and Ukraine—Treasury cited recommendations from the Financial Action Task Force (FATF), an international body whose purpose is the development and promotion of national and international policies to combat money laundering and terrorist financing as well as internal Treasury research and other sources, according to Treasury officials.

there are no requirements for it to designate time frames for when to complete the action and (2) agency officials were unclear about lines of authority designating which office within Treasury is responsible for finalizing or withdrawing proposed rules. The duration of a proposed rule was significant because, in all the cases we reviewed, U.S. financial institutions took immediate action on the basis of an announced finding and proposed restrictions, effectively implementing them before they were finalized.[7] Once a finding and notice of proposed rule-making are published in the *Federal Register*, interested parties have 30 days to provide written comments on the proposed rule to Treasury. The agency reviews the comments it receives, considers them in its decision to finalize or withdraw the proposed rule, and may sometimes meet with representatives of the targeted financial institution and foreign government to discuss their written comments or to receive additional information. However, Treasury has taken as long as 5 years to complete these actions for 1 of 11 cases and as little as 4 to 5 months for 4 cases. As of February 2008, it had not completed action on three cases, which had remained open for between 44 and 60 months beyond a 30-day comment period. By April 2008, Treasury withdrew two of the notices of proposed rule-making and officials said they are actively considering completing the third. Officials at one Treasury office, identified by its officials as being involved in making the determination to complete the Section 311 process, were not aware these cases were still open until we brought this to their attention. Officials of a second Treasury office, which Treasury attorneys identified as responsible for implementing Section 311, were aware that these three cases were open, as their status was listed on the office Web site, but these officials did not believe that they were responsible for finalizing or withdrawing them. Treasury officials said that it has no written guidance specifically on implementing Section 311 to clarify these responsibilities pursuant to management control standards.[8]

Treasury views Section 311 restrictions as effective, despite acknowledging concerns expressed by U.S. and foreign government officials, and representatives of financial institutions about the process. Section 311 restrictions are intended to achieve (1) the anti-money

---

[7]Financial institutions typically act immediately to comply with these proposed rules.

[8]Federal management control standards require that the agency's organizational structure clearly define key areas of authority and responsibility and establish appropriate lines of reporting. GAO, *Standards for Internal Control in the Federal Government*, GAO/AIMD-00-21.3.1 (Washington, D.C.: November 1999).

laundering goal of isolating target financial institutions from the U.S. financial system and (2) a broader national security goal of encouraging foreign governments to strengthen their anti-money laundering laws and regulations, according to Treasury officials. Treasury views Section 311 actions as effective in achieving the anti-money laundering goal because U.S. financial institutions responded immediately to notices that Treasury intended to issue a rule prohibiting them from continuing business with a targeted foreign institution. An immediate response makes good business sense to protect banks from risks to their reputation and possible government penalties. Treasury views Section 311 as effective in achieving the broader national security goal because several foreign governments have strengthened their anti-money laundering laws and regulations in response to Section 311 actions targeted against financial institutions in their jurisdictions. However, Treasury does not view concerns about Section 311's implementation as having an impact on the achievements of Section 311. For example, some foreign government officials we visited expressed concern with the implementation of Section 311 as not affording them an opportunity to bring their own law enforcement or regulatory actions against targeted financial institutions and not being given sufficient information to do so. Justice officials said that in cases where application of Section 311 is perceived as unsubstantiated, countries may be less likely to cooperate with the U.S. government on other sanctions or law enforcement matters.

We are recommending that the Secretary of the Treasury establish implementing guidance for Section 311 of the USA PATRIOT Act that would specify the responsibilities and activities of offices within Treasury for implementing and finalizing Section 311 actions.

Treasury said that it will take action to clarify its Section 311 processes in response to this report's recommendation, even though it emphasized that the current coordination and implementation of Section 311 within Treasury components today has been significantly improved. Although Treasury said that it has well-defined mechanisms in place to implement Section 311, it nonetheless stated that the Under Secretary of the Office of Terrorism and Financial Intelligence will ensure that mechanisms for implementing Section 311 are clarified in response to this report and its recommendation. Justice and State had no comments on this report.

Background

Section 311 is one of many legal and regulatory resources that the United States uses to combat money laundering and financial crime. U.S. laws and programs aimed at combating money laundering include the Bank Secrecy

Act (BSA), which includes Section 311 and authorizes Treasury to promulgate regulations on the reporting and recordkeeping of certain financial transactions; economic and trade sanctions implemented by the Office of Foreign Assets Control (OFAC); and several Justice programs focused on anti-money laundering. The United States is also a member of the Financial Action Task Force (FATF), an intergovernmental body that has created a comprehensive global framework for anti-money laundering efforts and has called for countermeasures against countries that are not complying with this framework.

These laws and programs, including Section 311, are part of a broad U.S. money laundering strategy. Issued most recently in 2007, this strategy states that it reflects the U.S. government's ongoing commitment to attack money laundering and terrorist financing on all fronts, including the formal and informal components of both the domestic and international financial systems.[9] The strategy focuses on three major goals: (1) to more effectively cut off access to the international financial system by money launderers and terrorist financiers; (2) to enhance the federal government's ability to target major money laundering organizations and systems; and (3) strengthen and refine the anti-money laundering regulatory regime for all financial institutions to improve the effectiveness of compliance and enforcement efforts. The strategy includes, among other items, a commitment to target countries and financial institutions that facilitate money laundering and terrorist financing, including using the full range of measures provided by Section 311 of the USA PATRIOT Act.

USA PATRIOT Act Section 311 is currently implemented by Treasury's Financial Crimes Enforcement Network (FinCEN). Until 2004, the Office of Terrorist Financing and Financial Crime (TFFC) implemented Section 311, according to Treasury officials. Both offices report to Treasury's Office of Terrorism and Financial Intelligence (TFI). This office contains intelligence and enforcement functions and has the stated twin missions of safeguarding the U.S. financial system against illicit use and combating national security threats. Figure 1 shows the organization of TFI.

---

[9]U.S. Department of the Treasury, U.S. Department of Justice, and U.S. Department of Homeland Security. The *2003 National Money Laundering Strategy*. This strategy was updated in 2007 as outlined in the *2007 National Money Laundering Strategy* (Washington, D.C.).

Figure 1: Organization of the Terrorism and Financial Intelligence Office

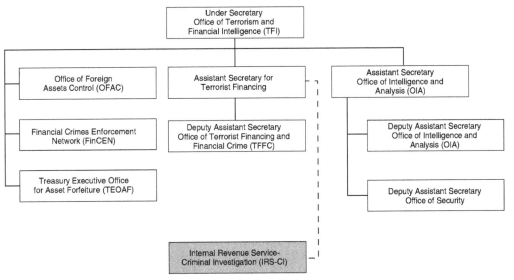

Source: Department of the Treasury.

Section 311 allows Treasury to require domestic financial institutions and agencies to take certain special measures outlined in the provision if it finds reasonable grounds to conclude that a designated foreign jurisdiction, financial institution, or class of transactions is of "primary money laundering concern."[10] In making a finding that a jurisdiction is of primary money laundering concern—in addition to any information that the Secretary of the Treasury might deem relevant—the Secretary is to consider seven potentially relevant factors. These additional factors include the extent to which the jurisdiction offers special bank secrecy or regulatory advantages to nonresidents as well as the substance and quality of the bank supervisory and anti-money laundering laws in the jurisdiction. In making a finding that an institution, transaction, or type of account is of primary money laundering concern, the Secretary is to consider–in addition to any information the Secretary determines is relevant–three potentially relevant factors, including the extent to which the institution is used to facilitate money laundering and the extent to which it is used to facilitate legitimate business. For a list of all potentially relevant factors

---

[10]All Section 311 actions applied as of the date of this report concerned jurisdictions or institutions only.

GAO-08-1058 USA Patriot Act

Treasury is required to consider, see appendix II. According to the law, the Secretary of the Treasury must consult with State and Justice before designating an institution, jurisdiction, or class of transactions is of primary money laundering concern.[11]

Once an institution is designated as being of primary money laundering concern, the Secretary of the Treasury is required to consult with a variety of parties including the Secretary of State, the Chairman of the Board of Governors of the Federal Reserve System, and other appropriate federal agencies,[12] to determine which of the five available special measures to apply. The first four special measures relate to requirements put on U.S. financial institutions or agencies for record keeping, reporting, and collection of certain financial information.[13] The fifth special measure prohibits U.S. financial institutions or agencies from opening or maintaining correspondent accounts or payable through accounts for or on behalf of a foreign bank if the account involves a designated jurisdiction or institution.[14] This special measure may be imposed only by regulation. In selecting which special measures to apply, the Secretary is required to consider four factors. These factors are listed in appendix III.

---

[11]Justice, State, and Treasury officials described this consultation role as reviewing and commenting on the evidence and documentation used to support a finding of primary money laundering concern.

[12]In addition, under Section 311, the Secretary of the Treasury is required to consult with the Securities and Exchange Commission, the Commodity Futures Trading Commission, the National Credit Union Administration Board, as well as other agencies and interested parties as the Secretary finds appropriate. Federal Reserve officials said that their agency's consultation role, and that of these other agencies, is to comment on technical language in the rule related to banking supervision, rather than to provide feedback on whether the finding is justified. Officials said that when reviewing a draft rule, the Federal Reserve considers (1) what the effect of the proposed rule will be on the banking industry and (2) whether the language in the rule is clear enough that its banks can easily understand and implement it.

[13]The first four special measures cover record keeping and reporting of certain financial transactions, collection of information relating to beneficial ownership, collection of information relating to certain payable through accounts, and collection of information relating to certain correspondent accounts.

[14]A payable through account is an account, including a transaction account, opened at a depository institution by a foreign financial institution by means of which the foreign financial institution permits its customers to engage, either directly or through a sub account, in banking activities usual in connection with the business of banking in the United States.

The Administrative Procedure Act, which governs federal rule-making, generally requires that notice of proposed rule-making be published in the Federal Register.[15] It also requires that, after the notice is given, the agency provide interested persons an opportunity to participate in the rule-making through submission of written data, views, or arguments. After consideration of these submissions, the agency is required to incorporate in the rules adopted a concise general statement of their basis and purpose.

Process to Implement USA PATRIOT Act Section 311 Was Consistent with Legal Requirements, but Some Agencies Expressed Concerns about Consultation

To implement USA PATRIOT Act Section 311, Treasury used an evolving informal rule-making process that was consistent with requirements in Section 311 and resulted in 11 cases in eight countries from 2002 through 2005. However, Treasury's process for consulting with two U.S. agencies on findings of primary money laundering concern sometimes made it difficult to provide meaningful consultation during certain key phases of the process, according to Justice and State officials. In the absence of established time frames, officials of these agencies expressed concerns about the amount of time they had for consultation about Section 311 findings. In addition, Treasury did not include these other agencies with expertise in money laundering and international affairs in developing its initial list of targeted financial institutions. Starting in 2006, Treasury changed its targeting procedures and, with Justice, established an interagency working group to discuss potential threats to the U.S. financial system at an earlier stage in the process. However, it is unclear whether the new procedures improved consultation because Treasury's current process has not resulted in any new Section 311 findings since 2005.

Treasury Developed Informal Rule-making Process to Implement USA PATRIOT Act Section 311

To implement USA PATRIOT Act Section 311, Treasury generally pursued the following steps from 2002 through 2005 that evolved over time:

---

[15]Regulatory proposals or proposed amendments to existing regulations are known as "proposed rules." Notices of public hearings or requests for comments on proposed rules are published in the *Federal Register*, on the Web sites of the regulatory agencies, and in newspapers and other publications. Once a regulation takes effect, it becomes a "final rule" and is printed in the *Federal Register*, the Code of Federal Regulations, and usually is posted on the Web site of the regulatory agency.

1. Identified target jurisdictions (countries) and financial institutions that presented a potential threat to the U.S. financial system because of money laundering or terrorist financing where Section 311 might be applied.

2. Conducted research to determine which of these jurisdictions or financial institutions were "of primary money laundering concern" and determined which special measures should be applied.

3. Drafted a finding and special measures, usually in a notice of proposed rule-making.

4. Reviewed the proposed rule for legal sufficiency.

5. Consulted with relevant agencies (Justice, State, the Federal Reserve, and other agencies) on a finding and the application of special measures.

6. Obtained clearance to proceed from Treasury's management.

7. Published a finding or notice of proposed rule-making in the Federal Register.

8. Received and reviewed comments.

9. Consulted, if applicable, with Justice, State, and the Federal Reserve, on the application of special measure 5.

10. Finalized or withdrew the proposed rule, as appropriate.

Treasury officials said that they had no single established process to implement Section 311, but developed informal rule-making processes that evolved over time. Prior to 2004, all work on Section 311 cases was conducted by the Office of Enforcement and was primarily the responsibility of Treasury's Deputy Assistant Secretary for Terrorist Financing and Financial Crime and his staff. At the beginning of 2004, Treasury officials told us a decision was made to move the function of building an administrative record of the supporting evidence associated with each Section 311 case and proposed rule to FinCEN. However, TFFC is still involved in making the determination of when a proposed rule should be published, finalized, or withdrawn, according to Treasury officials.

GAO-08-1058 USA Patriot Act

To date, Treasury has issued findings of primary money laundering concern against three jurisdictions and eight financial institutions in eight countries. The first finding of primary money laundering concern was issued in December 2002 and the most recent finding occurred in September 2005. The three countries in these findings were: (1) Ukraine, (2) Nauru, and (3) Burma. The eight financial institutions in these findings were: (1) Asia Wealth Bank (Burma), (2) Myanmar Mayflower Bank (Burma), (3) Commercial Bank of Syria (Syria), (4) First Merchant Bank OSH Ltd. (Turkish Cyprus),[16] (5) Belmetalnergo/Infobank (Belarus), (6) Multibanka (Latvia), (7) VEF Banka (Latvia), and (8) Banco Delta Asia (Macau, China).

In all of the cases above, Treasury issued a designation of primary money laundering concern. In all cases but one,[17] Treasury also issued proposed rules regarding the institution or jurisdiction designated to be of primary money laundering concern. These rules proposed that U.S. financial institutions employ Special Measure 5, prohibiting U.S. financial institutions covered by the rule from opening or maintaining correspondent accounts with foreign banks if the account involved designated institutions or jurisdictions. Of the 10 proposed rules it issued under Section 311, Treasury later withdrew 3 and finalized 6, with one rule still outstanding. For additional information on these countries and financial institutions, see appendix IV.

Treasury Identified Targeted Institutions Where Section 311 Might be Applied

To implement the key first step of targeting areas of primary money laundering concern, according to Treasury officials, Treasury identified jurisdictions and financial institutions from several sources. These were multilateral organization recommendations, U.S. law enforcement investigations, joint strategy with State, and broader national security concerns.

For the jurisdictions it targeted from 2002 through 2005—the countries of Burma, Nauru, and Ukraine—Treasury officials said they relied largely on

---

[16]Subsidiaries of this bank included First Merchant Finance Ltd., First Merchant International Inc., First Merchant Trust Ltd., and FMB Finance Ltd.

[17]For Ukraine, Treasury issued a finding and announced its intention to issue a proposed rule applying special measures 1 through 4. However, Treasury did not issue a proposed rule and withdrew the finding against Ukraine 4 months later, based on Ukraine's passing anti-money laundering legislation, its commitment to implement this legislation, and the FATF's decision to rescind a call for countermeasures against Ukraine.

GAO-08-1058 USA Patriot Act

recommendations from the FATF, an international body whose purpose is the development and promotion of national and international policies to combat money laundering and terrorist financing, as well as on internal Treasury research and other sources. The first opportunity to use Section 311 arose out of the FATF's Non-Cooperative Countries and Territories (NCCT) process, according to Treasury officials. Once a country was placed on the NCCT list, FATF member states, including the United States, had an obligation to advise financial institutions in their country to give enhanced scrutiny to financial transactions with financial institutions on the FATF NCCT list. If after a year, a country had not taken the appropriate measures to be removed from the NCCT list, then FATF would request that its member countries place additional countermeasures against the country, according to Treasury officials. Treasury officials told us that prior to the passage of Section 311, the United States had no real countermeasures to impose on countries when FATF called for them. After Section 311 was passed, Treasury decided to use the provision in response to the FATF's call for additional country countermeasures. In early 2000, FATF called for countermeasures against Ukraine and Nauru and, in 2003, called for countermeasures against Burma. Subsequently, Treasury responded by invoking Section 311 against all three countries, according to Treasury officials.

For financial institutions it targeted, Treasury used a different approach from that used for jurisdictions. It developed a list of possible targets for the purpose of using the new Section 311 authority, according to U.S. government officials. In 2002 and 2003, Treasury officials said, the Office of Enforcement, which preceded TFFC, assigned each of its five to six staff to review a region of the world in order to review intelligence reports and identify potential targets in each region. Ultimately, the office produced a list of over 20 banks of money laundering concern that were potential targets for Section 311 action. Treasury officials told us that their offices developed the list of targeted financial institutions internally. While Treasury officials said that they did not consult other agency officials with expertise in money laundering and international affairs in developing the initial list of targets, Treasury developed the list from various sources, based on material developed by other agencies.

Treasury officials identified several sources as the impetus for its findings of primary money-laundering concern for various financial institutions.

- The finding against one bank occurred because there was an ongoing FBI investigation of the bank, according to Treasury officials. They said that this case was the first opportunity Treasury had to use Section 311 in conjunction with law enforcement.

- The findings against two other banks emerged from a concern that a foreign government was not reforming its anti-money laundering laws, according to Treasury officials. They said that the U.S. government had been concerned for some time with lack of anti-money laundering controls in the country, but had not pursued the issue until it became apparent that anti-money laundering controls were not going to be addressed. At that point, Treasury met with State to develop a strategy for dealing with the country's anti-money laundering control issues. Following the Section 311 finding, the foreign government passed legislation to improve its national anti-money laundering controls.

- The findings against two other targeted banks emerged from several national security working groups and were part of a higher National Security Council strategy for these particular countries, according to Treasury officials.

After developing the target list, Treasury conducted research to support a finding for each targeted institution on the list. If it determined that it had enough evidence to support a Section 311 finding, it published a proposed rule in the Federal Register identifying the institution as being of "primary money laundering concern."

Treasury Process for Implementing Section 311 Was Consistent with Legal Requirements

Treasury's process for implementing Section 311 was consistent with requirements set forth in the USA PATRIOT Act. From 2002 through 2005, in accordance with USA PATRIOT Act Section 311, Treasury generally considered the seven factors outlined in Section 311 when determining whether a jurisdiction is of primary money laundering concern, including the quality of bank supervision and anti-money laundering laws in the jurisdiction. For example, for the jurisdiction of Burma, Treasury found that Burma lacked a basic set of anti-money laundering laws and that the Burmese Central Bank had no anti-money laundering regulations for financial institutions. For proposed rules determining whether an institution was of primary money laundering concern, Treasury considered the three factors outlined in Section 311 for financial institutions. For example, Treasury determined that the Commercial Bank of Syria was being used to facilitate or promote money laundering because numerous transactions were indicative of money laundering passed through that bank. Treasury also determined that any legitimate business activity at the bank was significantly outweighed by the apparent use of the bank to promote money laundering.

When determining which special measures to apply under Section 311, Treasury considered the four factors required by the law. For example, Treasury considered whether similar action was being taken by other nations or organizations, the burden of special measures for U.S. financial institution compliance, the impact of special measures on the international financial system, and the effect of special measures on U.S. national security and foreign policy when it announced Section 311 special measures for Banco Delta Asia. Appendix II provides a more detailed description of these factors. In addition, consistent with Section 311 of the USA Patriot Act, Treasury's process for instituting special measure 5 was imposed only through rule-making.

Two Agencies Noted Limited Opportunities to Contribute Their Views

While Treasury met the statutory requirements of USA PATRIOT Act Section 311 to consult with designated agencies, Justice and State officials expressed concerns with the amount of time they had for consultation about Section 311 findings in the absence of established time frames.

Officials of two U.S. agencies expressed concerns about the amount of time they had for consulting with Treasury on Section 311 cases prior to issuing proposed rules. Before a proposed rule was issued for public comment, Treasury provided it to Justice and State for consultation, as required by the act.[18] Though the consultations fulfilled requirements under Section 311, Justice and State officials said that consultations often occurred under short time frames, affording them insufficient opportunity to provide meaningful input to the Section 311 process. Treasury established no operational guidance with set time frames for this consultation requirement. For example, one Justice official stated that Justice generally received an e-mail from Treasury asking Justice if it wanted to comment on a proposed rule and setting very tight time

---

[18]In making a finding that reasonable grounds exist for concluding that a jurisdiction, financial institution, transaction, or type of account is of primary money laundering concern the Secretary of the Treasury is required to consult with the Secretary of State and the Attorney General. When selecting special measures, the Secretary of the Treasury is required to consult with the Chairman of the Board of Governors of the Federal Reserve System, any other appropriate federal banking agencies, the Secretary of State, the Securities and Exchange Commission, the Commodity Futures Trading Commission, the National Credit Union Administration Board, and in the sole discretion of the Secretary, such other agencies and interested parties as the Secretary may find to be appropriate.

frames—in one case as little as 1 to 2 days—with no explanation as to why time frames were so tight. Other Justice officials said that the short time frame required that most of the feedback from Justice to Treasury was oral, but that in one case neither Justice nor Treasury had access to a Sensitive Compartmented Information Facility to discuss classified information during the time period provided. As a result, all conversations between the two agencies needed to be general and could not be classified. This was problematic because one Justice official said that most of Justice's comments regarded evidence that was highly classified. Also, short time frames made consultation difficult because they did not allow the relevant Justice official who had reviewed the classified evidence time to collect comments or concerns from other officials in Justice.

Treasury officials disagreed with concerns expressed about their consultation roles. They stated their belief that Treasury coordinates extensively. Treasury worked with other agencies on various cases. For example, in one case, Treasury worked for months with the intelligence agencies in developing the case and with State, including the Secretary of State, on the designation, according to the officials. Treasury officials said that they also consulted with State's Undersecretary for Economic and Business Affairs as required. In addition, Treasury officials said that they delayed one case because of law enforcement interests in the targeted institution and that law enforcement equities are a primary concern for Treasury. Moreover, Treasury said that it has accommodated other agencies' concerns and always ensured that it did not endanger the operational interests of law enforcement and the intelligence community. Treasury stated that it had never gone forward with Section 311 actions without consultation or over the objections of other agencies.

Treasury Changed Its Process for Implementing Section 311

In early 2006, FinCEN changed Section 311 procedures in order to make better use of the staff's time, according to a Treasury official. Targeted assessments of financial institutions that may be of primary money laundering concern are now prepared instead of complete Section 311 packages. This is because preparing a complete package took considerable time, according to this official, and then had to be assessed to determine if there was sufficient evidence to justify a finding and proposed rule. The process now begins when a request for preparing an assessment comes from either (1) within FinCEN, based on a daily FinCEN review of intelligence and public materials looking for threats to the U.S. financial system or (2) other parts of Treasury or other agencies with suggestions for a targeted assessment. In deciding whether or not to prepare a targeted assessment, FinCEN first considers whether an

GAO-08-1058 USA Patriot Act

institution has access to the U.S. financial system. If not, FinCEN takes no action to assess it. Once an assessment is prepared, it is presented either to the Under Secretary for Terrorism and Financial Intelligence or to the Director of FinCEN, or both, for a policy decision on whether further action should be taken. None of the targeted assessments has resulted in Section 311 actions, but Treasury said it has selected other options to address these threats.

The second change in the implementation process was the formation of an interagency working group to review suspect banks. This group developed over time but formally began meeting in January 2008. According to the Chief of Justice's Asset Forfeiture & Money Laundering Section (AFMLS), he developed an informal working relationship with Treasury, primarily through meetings with the Deputy Assistant Secretary of TFFC, on a monthly or bimonthly basis. This evolved into a working group to review suspect banks for possible anti-money laundering efforts, including Section 311 actions. This process was formalized in the first 6 months of 2008 and the working group has met about 6 times. The Deputy Assistant Secretary for TFFC at Treasury noted that this group gives the Section 311 process a broader perspective on suspect banks. The Chief of Justice's AFMLS section also said that this working group is a significant improvement over Treasury's previous process for identifying banks for possible Section 311 action, which had not been clear to Justice officials. The working group also allows Justice to learn about possible Section 311 actions early, thus alerting Justice to actions that could impact ongoing covert operations. The Justice official noted that one of its goals for the working group is to maintain anti-money laundering expertise and a law enforcement perspective, since TFFC is not a law enforcement agency. The Justice official emphasized that the group has good potential but that it will take another 6 months to see how well it works.

Membership in the suspect banks' working group consists of a wide variety of organizations. The Chief of Justice's AFMLS co-chairs the group with Treasury's Deputy Assistant Secretary for TFFC. Other members of the group are State (representatives from its division of International Narcotics and Law Enforcement bureau); staff from TFFC and FinCEN, and the international division at Treasury; and components of the intelligence community. These agencies are the core group that now attends all meetings, but other agencies may be also asked to attend specific meetings. State was not initially at the first meetings of the working group but had been invited after the first few meetings when it became clear that its input was needed.

Treasury's Process for Implementing Section 311 Followed Requirements of the Law but Took Years to Finalize Some Proposed Rules

It has sometimes taken Treasury years to finalize or withdraw a proposed Section 311 rule, though these delays are not inconsistent with requirements under the law. This has occurred, in part because (1) there are no requirements to designate time frames for completing actions and (2) Treasury officials were unclear about which office in Treasury was responsible for finalizing or withdrawing proposed rules. Nonetheless, the Section 311 proposed rules had a significant impact because U.S. financial institutions took immediate action on the basis of their being announced, effectively implementing them before they were finalized.

Treasury's Timeline for Issuing Proposed and Final Rules Follows Requirements in the Administrative Procedure Act

Though sometimes delayed, Treasury's process for issuing proposed and final rules follows requirements in the Administrative Procedure Act.[19] The Administrative Procedure Act generally requires that agencies issue a proposed rule in the Federal Register and that they give interested persons an opportunity to participate in rule-making through the submission of written data, views, or arguments. Treasury officials said they reviewed all comments they received in response to proposed rules. Officials said that in some cases, they also met with affected financial institutions at the institutions' request. Treasury then determines whether to finalize or withdraw a proposed rule. This step is important because, in contrast to a proposed rule, a final rule imposes legal requirements on U.S. financial institutions. However, rule-making requirements of the Administrative Procedure Act do not place any time frames on officials specifying by when a proposed rule must be finalized or withdrawn.[20]

---

[19]In the two earliest uses of Section 311 cases, Treasury first issued findings of money laundering concern prior to making a determination as to whether to issue a proposed rule. In one of these cases (Nauru) it followed this finding with a proposed rule. In the other case (Ukraine), Treasury rescinded the finding of primary money laundering concern.

[20]See 5 U.S.C. § 553.

Treasury Took Years to Finalize Some Proposed Rules

In some cases, Treasury took years to finalize proposed rules. For example, as of February 2008, 3 of the 11 cases it had opened still had not been finalized, with two open for more than 3 years (44 and 49 months, respectively) and one open for 5 years (60 months). These cases contrast sharply with other Section 311 cases where Treasury took as little as 4 months to follow up on a finding of primary money laundering concern or a proposed rule. Figure 2 shows the length of time proposed rules were open for all Section 311 actions. Additional information on the date of issuance of findings of primary money laundering concern, proposed rules, and final rules for all Section 311 actions is in appendix IV.

Figure 2: Length of Time to Finalize or Withdraw Proposed Section 311 Rules

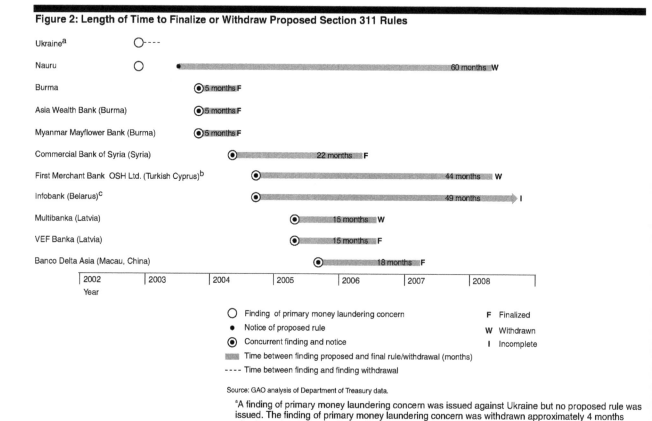

Source: GAO analysis of Department of Treasury data.

[a]A finding of primary money laundering concern was issued against Ukraine but no proposed rule was issued. The finding of primary money laundering concern was withdrawn approximately 4 months after it was issued on April 17, 2003, based on Ukrainian passage of anti-money laundering legislation, its commitment to implement this legislation, and the FATF's decision to rescind a call for countermeasures against Ukraine.

Treasury lacks operational guidance and clear lines of authority for finalizing proposed rules, which may have contributed to the length of time it took to do so. Federal government management control standards require that agencies have policies and procedures for implementing management directives and that agencies clearly define key areas of responsibility throughout their organization.[21] However, Treasury does not have policies and procedures that provide operational guidance as to when proposed rules should be finalized or other procedures that Treasury staff should follow when implementing Section 311 actions. In addition, we observed that there are not clear lines of responsibility as to which office within Treasury should finalize these proposed rules.

Treasury officials said that they follow the law and rule-making procedures outlined in the Administrative Procedure Act when implementing proposed rules. However, as mentioned earlier, the law provides no time frames to which officials are expected to adhere between the issuance of a notice of proposed rule-making and a final rule. Instead, Treasury officials told us that the events that occur in a case and the priorities of the office implementing the rule affect the amount of time that elapses between when a rule is proposed and when it is finalized. For example, one FinCEN official said that his work on finalizing a proposed rule was delayed when another Section 311 case became a higher priority. The proposed rule in this case was eventually finalized after more than 3 years.

Several additional factors accounted for the interval of time between issuing findings and proposed rules and finalizing or withdrawing them. Staff at FinCEN said that often the decision to postpone a case is made simply because there are not enough resources to concentrate on all of the cases at hand. For example, one official said that he was working on resolving the proposed rule-making for one bank when another case began. Once the second case became a priority, work on the first was put on hold so that all staff could work on the other case, since only a few staff within FinCEN work on Section 311 cases, according to the official.

---

[21]GAO/AIMD-00-21.3.1 (Washington, D.C.: November 1999).

In addition, Treasury officials said, they extended a comment period for two banks, while in another case, they postponed final action on an institution for several months pending completion of a law enforcement investigation. Also contributing to the interval between a proposed rule and a final or withdrawn rule is that Treasury monitors financial institutions on an ad hoc basis after a proposed rule is issued. For example, in one case FinCEN required several months in 2007 to confirm whether banks under Section 311 restrictions were still in business and an additional 9 months to withdraw the proposed rule after receiving the information.

Treasury officials' uncertainty about clear lines of responsibility added to delays in finalizing proposed rules. Both FinCEN and TFFC officials told us Treasury has prepared no written guidance outlining the responsibilities of each bureau for administering Section 311. In addition, it appears that the bureaus have not determined their respective responsibilities in finalizing proposed rules. For example, in February 2008, three proposed rules were open, with two having been open for more than 4 years beyond the 30-day comment period. Senior TFFC officials were not aware that these cases were still open until we brought this fact to their attention. In contrast to TFFC, FinCEN officials were aware that these cases were open, as their status was listed on FinCEN's website. In addition, a lack of clear lines of responsibility led to confusion over the responsibility for closing these cases. FinCEN officials did not believe that they were responsible for closing them. They stated that TFI is responsible for deciding when to decide to finalize or withdraw a proposed rule, although FinCEN staff may sometimes take the initiative to suggest that a rule be finalized or postponed. TFFC officials, on the other hand, said that FinCEN was responsible for finalizing proposed rules. TFFC officials followed up on the proposed rules that were outstanding after we discussed the rules with them.[22] Although Treasury stated that it had started action to withdraw two of the proposed rules prior to our discussion with TFFC, Treasury documents showed that FinCEN previously had started to draft a withdrawal notice for one case in 2005 but never completed it, and had started again in October 2007 to draft withdrawal notices for this and a second case, before issuing them 6 months later.

---

[22]Two of these proposed rules were subsequently withdrawn in April 2008. One proposed rule is still incomplete, but Treasury officials said they are currently consulting with other agencies about whether to issue a final rule.

GAO-08-1058 USA Patriot Act

In response to our observation of unclear lines of authority, senior FinCEN and TFFC officials said that, pursuant to law and a related Treasury order, FinCEN is the administrator of the BSA, of which USA PATRIOT Act amendments are a part. Therefore, FinCEN is technically responsible for administering Section 311. The Treasury officials added that FinCEN coordinates closely with TFFC on all aspects of Section 311 rule-making.

Proposed Rules Had an Immediate Impact on Targeted Countries and Financial Institutions

Despite taking years to finalize in some cases, proposed rules under Section 311 had an immediate impact on targeted institutions and jurisdictions. Treasury, State, and Justice officials told us that once a proposed rule is issued, almost all U.S. financial institutions immediately implement it voluntarily, stopping financial transactions with designated financial institutions or jurisdictions. Federal Reserve and Treasury's Office of the Comptroller of the Currency officials also said that U.S. banks often treat proposed Section 311 rules as final and generally cut off all financial interactions with the targeted institution. Federal Reserve officials noted that this response to a proposed rule is unusual and, within the context of BSA requirements, appears to be unique to proposed rules under Section 311. Officials explained that U.S. banks may be taking this action because the proposed rule is associated with a finding of primary money laundering concern and, in many instances, Treasury issued a finding together with a notice of proposed rule-making. Because it makes good business sense to protect banks from risks to their reputation and possible government penalties, banks may discontinue business with other banks labeled a primary money laundering concern to reduce their reputational risk. Banks may be concerned that continuing business with a bank labeled as of "primary money laundering concern" would negatively impact their reputation. Moreover, U.S. financial institutions must take publicly available information into account when implementing their anti-money laundering programs and assessing risks. In addition, banks are generally given a short time frame to come into compliance with rules under Section 311 once they are finalized, so they may cut off all financial interaction with a targeted entity when the proposed rule is issued to ensure that they have minimized their risk of non-compliance.

Foreign government officials and representatives from targeted financial institutions in countries we visited also agreed that proposed rules have an immediate impact on these institutions and jurisdictions. Foreign government officials told us that, following the issuance of proposed rules, U.S. correspondent accounts of targeted banks were immediately closed. Bank representatives also told us that the proposed rules had a significant impact on their business. Bank managers from one targeted institution stated that the banks' deposits had decreased by one third of their original amount 3 days after the proposed rule was issued. In another case, a bank lost approximately 80 percent of its business as a result of a proposed rule, according to a bank representative. Attorneys for targeted financial institutions with whom we spoke emphasized that the amount of time between the proposed and final rule is important to targeted institutions since a long delay can weaken a bank financially. One legal representative noted that long delays between the proposed and final rule can put a bank in a financial position where it cannot afford to take legal action in U.S. court opposing special measures if a rule is finalized against it.

Treasury Views Section 311 as Effective, despite Concerns Expressed by Others about the Process

Treasury views Section 311 restrictions as effective, despite concerns expressed by others about the process. Section 311 restrictions are intended to achieve (1) the anti-money laundering goal of isolating target financial institutions from the U.S. financial system and (2) a broader national security goal of encouraging foreign governments to strengthen their anti-money laundering laws and regulations, according to Treasury officials. Treasury views Section 311 actions as effective in achieving both goals because U.S. financial institutions respond immediately to proposed rules, and several foreign governments have strengthened their laws and regulations in response to proposed rules. However, Treasury does not view the long-term impact of proposed and final rules, including negative foreign perceptions of their implementation, as outweighing the observable achievements of Section 311.

U.S. Agencies and Foreign Governments View Section 311 as Effective

U.S. and foreign government officials with whom we spoke said that they consider Section 311 to be an effective anti-money laundering tool and to have had a significant impact on target financial institutions and countries. According to Treasury officials, Section 311 restrictions are intended to achieve (1) the anti-money laundering goal of isolating target financial institutions from the U.S. financial system and (2) a broader national security goal of encouraging foreign governments to strengthen their anti-money laundering laws and regulations.

Several U.S. government officials said that Section 311 was effective in achieving the first goal of isolating targeted financial institutions or jurisdictions from the U.S. financial system. For example, one State official said that the imposition of Section 311 was very effective for the majority of countries targeted because financial systems in other countries were so closely tied to the U.S. financial system. Generally, the imposition of a

Section 311 action, beginning with the issuance of a proposed rule, caused U.S. banks to voluntarily cut off transactions with the targeted financial institutions even when proposed rules were not finalized. In addition, the action has a chilling effect on foreign investment through the bank or in the country because the banking industry pays close attention to the actions of U.S. financial institutions, according to the official.

Several U.S. and foreign government officials said that Section 311 was effective in achieving the second goal because it influenced some foreign governments to strengthen their anti-money laundering laws and regulations. Officials specifically cited the Latvia, Macau, and Ukraine cases as examples of this. For example, one Treasury official noted that, after the Section 311 action occurred, the government of Latvia worked closely with the U.S. Embassy and State to address problems related to financial crime which had caused Treasury to issue the Section 311 findings. While foreign government officials in these countries did not dispute the statement, some said either that their governments had already started to strengthen their laws and regulations when the Section 311 action occurred, or that they had responded as much or more to other actions, such as the FATF call for countermeasures, than to the U.S. restrictions.

Concerns about Section 311 Exist Both in the United States and Abroad

Despite the achievements observed from initial monitoring of Section 311 actions, we identified several concerns about the impact of Section 311's implementation. U.S. embassy officials with whom we spoke and representatives of one targeted institution indicated that the impact of the proposed rule continued on the institution and the country even after the rule had been withdrawn. A number of U.S. banks have avoided holding correspondent bank accounts with any banks in the country since the Section 311 restriction was issued, according to embassy officials. They noted that the issuance of Section 311 creates a large stigma against banking with both the targeted banks under the proposed rule and other banks in the country where the proposed rule was targeted. Embassy officials said that several U.S. businessmen in the country have been told by U.S. bankers that they decided to withdraw from doing business in the country because of the Section 311 action. Foreign banking officials stated that the proposed rule continued to impact the country even though it was not targeted at the country specifically, and the United States had acknowledged the government's efforts in the anti-money laundering arena. One representative of a foreign institution pointed out that the consequences of Section 311 action against his country continue and may not have been intended. For example, American banks continue to be hesitant to do business with his country's banks and many have cut off business altogether. The official said that he believes this is because American banks do not believe that guidelines are clear as to what anti-money laundering standards they should be following. In order to minimize the risk of noncompliance with their regulators, many banks have stopped business with his country's banks altogether, regardless of whether they believe that a bank is following U.S. anti-money laundering standards.

Foreign regulatory and law enforcement agencies in some countries we visited said that how Section 311 actions were implemented did not provide them sufficient opportunity or information from U.S. government sources to prosecute crimes or regulate the targeted banks. For example, foreign government officials in one country that we visited noted that there were many steps that the government's monetary authority could have undertaken to put pressure on the targeted institution to improve its anti-money laundering controls. These actions might have solved the problem to the extent that the U.S. government would not have had to take action, according to the officials. The officials said that the monetary authority has the ability to obtain information from financial institutions, attach conditions to institutional operation, work with the Financial Intelligence Unit[23] to investigate financial crimes, and, in more drastic situations, appoint an advisor or director to take over a private bank. Treasury officials said that it discussed Section 311 actions with foreign government representatives when appropriate and provided ample notice that a Section 311 action was forthcoming in some cases. In some instances, however, such communications would be inappropriate, according to Treasury officials. Treasury officials noted that it is obligated under the USA PATRIOT Act to consider "the extent to which that jurisdiction is characterized by high levels of official or institutional corruption" when making a finding that a jurisdiction is of primary money laundering concern.

Justice officials said that in cases where application of Section 311 is perceived as unsubstantiated, it harms the United States. Countries may be less likely to cooperate with the U.S. government on other sanctions or law enforcement matters if they feel that the United States is acting in an unreasonable or unsubstantiated manner regarding Section 311 or that the

---

[23]Financial Intelligence Units are special government agencies that were created in several countries around the world to deal with the problem of money laundering.

United States cannot articulate the standards used to reach such a decision. In addition, when countries distrust actions the United States has taken under Section 311, their trust in U.S. actions in other areas is undermined. A Justice official noted that there are times when Justice needs to request the assistance of others based on classified information and sometimes it cannot immediately reveal this information or its source. In these cases, Justice needs foreign governments to trust the United States and act on its requests. If trust in the U.S. government has been eroded due to actions that appear to be unsubstantiated, then foreign governments may be less likely to cooperate with Justice investigations.

In addition, some U.S. government officials, foreign government officials, and representatives of banks in countries we visited, characterized the imposition of Section 311 special measures as a "political tool" and as sanctions. They saw Section 311 actions to be more like unilateral U.S. sanctions used for political purposes than law enforcement mechanisms used for anti-money laundering purposes.[24] Some similarities between Section 311 actions and sanctions—such as their being unilateral, designation of targeted persons or institutions, announcement of these designations in the Federal Register, prohibition of certain financial transactions, and denial of access to the U.S. financial system for designated parties—may contribute to this perception. Also, an official of Treasury's Office of the Comptroller of the Currency said that the only other process in his view that was similar to the Section 311 process is Treasury's OFAC sanctions process. Under such sanctions, according to the official, banks also automatically stop doing business with an institution once it is cited.

Treasury officials acknowledge that this perception exists but maintain that Section 311 is an anti-money laundering mechanism, not a sanction. In

[24]A U.S. "sanction" is any unilateral restriction or condition on economic activity with respect to a foreign country or foreign entity that is imposed by the United States for reasons of foreign policy or national security. For example, financial sanctions may be targeted against persons designated as either weapons of mass destruction proliferators or global terrorists, depending on which set of sanctions is employed, and any transactions with them by U.S. persons are prohibited. According to Treasury, the goal of this action is to deny sanctioned parties' access to the U.S. financial and commercial systems. Treasury or State can make designations under these financial sanctions, which are published in the *Federal Register*.

testimony in April 2008,[25] the Under Secretary of the Treasury for Terrorism and Financial Intelligence stated:

> Treasury adopted a new strategy of using targeted, conduct-based financial measures aimed at particular bad actors. I intentionally refer to these targeted actions as "financial measures" rather than "sanctions" because the word "sanctions" often evokes such a negative reaction. These targeted financial measures are proving to be quite effective, flying in the face of a widely-held historical view that dismisses sanctions as ineffective, harmful to innocents, or both. In the case of broad, country-wide sanctions that are often perceived as political statements, it can be difficult to persuade other governments and private businesses to join us in taking action.

Treasury reiterated its view that Section 311 actions are not sanctions despite the perception that they are by some U.S. officials and foreign governments. Senior Treasury officials regularly work to educate the public and foreign governments that these actions are not sanctions, according to Treasury officials. Treasury's OFAC administers the U.S. sanctions programs, which operate under very different authorities.

Finally, some U.S. government officials and foreign government officials we met with in countries where financial institutions had been targeted felt that there were several financial institutions of greater money laundering concern that had not been targeted and suggested that Treasury targeted financial institutions that were politically expedient rather than financial institutions that were of the greatest concern. For example, officials we spoke with about two countries we visited where financial institutions were identified for Section 311 actions told us that other banks in those countries had anti-money laundering controls that were as bad as, or worse than the banks that were targeted. They noted that it was not clear why Treasury chose the banks it chose as targets for Section 311 action. Treasury officials explained that it was important for Treasury to have flexibility in implementing Section 311 and that Treasury could have targeted other banks in one country, for example, that were larger than those it targeted. However, Treasury did not want to undermine the country's financial system but that, by selecting the smaller banks, it would still send the message to government authorities that they needed to reform the country's anti-money laundering systems.

---

[25]Testimony before the Senate Committee on Finance, Under Secretary for Terrorism and Financial Intelligence Stuart Levey (Washington, D.C.: Apr. 1, 2008).

GAO-08-1058 USA Patriot Act

Conclusion

U.S. government officials consider Section 311 to be an effective tool in restricting access to the U.S. financial markets for financial institutions or jurisdictions that are of primary money laundering concern and in encouraging foreign governments to strengthen their anti-money laundering laws and regulations. While using Section 311 has helped achieve success towards these goals in specific instances, shortcomings in Treasury's implementation of the law may be preventing the law from achieving a greater potential. Without written operational guidelines to clarify when to complete the Section 311 actions or clear lines of authority for which office is responsible for completing the action, Treasury has taken years to complete the Section 311 process for certain cases. Because a proposed rule applying Section 311 in practice has had the same effect as a final rule, Treasury may lack incentive to finalize or withdraw such rules. More expeditious completion of Section 311 cases could be an important counterbalance to concerns about the Section 311 process by affected jurisdictions, financial institutions, and other parties.

Recommendation for Executive Action

In order to improve implementation of the Section 311 process, we recommend that the Secretary of the Treasury establish implementing guidance for Section 311 of the USA PATRIOT Act. This guidance should specify the responsibilities and activities of offices within Treasury, including the Office of Terrorist Financing and Financial Crime and the Financial Crimes Enforcement Network, for implementing and finalizing Section 311 actions.

Agency Comments and Our Evaluation

We provided a draft of this report to Justice, State, and Treasury. Justice and State had no comments on this report.

Treasury said that it will take action to clarify its Section 311 processes in response to this report's recommendation, even though it emphasized that the current coordination and implementation of Section 311 within Treasury components today has been significantly improved. It noted that some of the report's conclusions were based on actions that occurred years ago and that current coordination and implementation of Section 311 within components of Treasury's Office of Terrorism and Financial Intelligence have addressed those actions. Although Treasury said that it has well-defined mechanisms in place to implement Section 311, it nonetheless stated that the Under Secretary of the Office of Terrorism and Financial Intelligence will ensure that mechanisms for implementing Section 311 are clarified in response to this report and its recommendation.

We appreciate Treasury's commitment to continuously improve the implementation of Section 311 as an important tool against money laundering and believe this is responsive to our recommendation regarding the need to specify the responsibilities and activities of offices within Treasury for implementing and finalizing Section 311 actions. As our report noted, Treasury has modified the Section 311 process since its inception, and the current process for its use differs in some significant ways from the process that Treasury used for previous Section 311 cases. We have made some additional modifications in our report to reflect technical comments that Treasury provided for clarification.

As agreed with your offices, unless you publicly announce the contents of this report earlier, we plan no further distribution until 30 days from the report date. At that time, we will send copies to interested congressional committees, and the U.S. Attorney General, and the Secretaries of State and Treasury. We will also make copies available to others upon request. In addition, this report will be available at no charge on the GAO Web site at http://www.gao.gov. If you or your staff has any questions concerning this report, please contact me at (202) 512-4347 or at yagerl@gao.gov. Contact points for our Office of Congressional Relations and Public Affairs may be found on the last page of this report. Staff acknowledgments are listed in appendix VI.

Loren Yager
Director, International Affairs and Trade

List of Requesters

The Honorable Ileana Ros-Lehtinen
Ranking Member
Committee on Foreign Affairs
House of Representatives

The Honorable Christopher H. Smith
Ranking Member
Subcommittee on Africa and Global Health
Committee on Foreign Affairs
House of Representatives

The Honorable Mike Pence
Ranking Member
Subcommittee on the Middle East
    and South Asia
Committee on Foreign Affairs
House of Representatives

The Honorable Edward R. Royce
Ranking Member
Subcommittee on Terrorism, Nonproliferation
    and Trade
Committee on Foreign Affairs
House of Representatives

The Honorable Dan Burton
Ranking Member
Subcommittee on the Western Hemisphere
Committee on Foreign Affairs
House of Representatives

The Honorable Joseph R. Pitts
House of Representatives

Appendix I: Scope and Methodology

To examine the process U.S. agencies used to implement the USA PATRIOT Act Section 311 restrictions against targeted financial institutions and countries, we interviewed knowledgeable officials from the Treasury offices of Terrorist Financing and Financial Crimes (TFFC) and the Financial Crimes Enforcement Network (FinCEN), as well as officials from State, Justice, and the U.S. Federal Reserve System who had been involved in the Section 311 process. We reviewed Section 311 of the USA PATRIOT Act and the Administrative Procedure Act in order to identify mandated requirements in law that Treasury must follow when it issues and finalizes a proposed rule. We focused this performance audit on locations where the U.S. government has targeted financial institutions or jurisdictions for Section 311 actions. These were Belarus, Burma, Latvia, Macau, Nauru, Syria, Turkish Republic of Northern Cyprus, and Ukraine. We also met with foreign government officials in Riga Latvia; Kyiv, Ukraine; and Macau and Hong Kong, China; as well as with representatives of financial institutions in these countries that had been targeted for Section 311 actions. These countries provided examples of different applications of Section 311, specifically a targeted jurisdiction and targeted financial institutions where Section 311 restrictions were finalized and withdrawn. We developed a data collection instrument for Treasury to more quickly identify relevant documents, including memoranda and emails. This helped us confirm that Treasury followed the steps in its Section 311 process for each of the cases for Belarus, Burma, Latvia, Macau, Nauru, Syria, Turkish Republic of Northern Cyprus, and Ukraine. We also reviewed unclassified and classified documents, including financial and investigative records, that Treasury compiled in its evidentiary files for each case; State cable traffic and its annual International Control Strategy Report on money laundering and financial crimes; and reports and guidance issued by the multinational Financial Action Task Force.

To assess the process Treasury used to determine whether to finalize or withdraw a proposed rule, we interviewed knowledgeable officials from TFFC and FinCEN, as well as officials from State, Justice, and the Federal Reserve who were involved in the 311 process. We also discussed this aspect of the Section 311 process with representatives of relevant financial institutions in New York and Washington, D.C.; Riga, Latvia; Kyiv, Ukraine; and Macau, China. We reviewed public comments on proposed rules that were issued under USA PATRIOT Act, Section 311. We also met with officials of Ernst and Young, and Deloitte Touche Tomatsu, two independent audit organizations that were hired by targeted financial institutions to help them reform their anti-money laundering controls. We reviewed documents identified by Treasury through our document collection instrument as being key documents related to the implementation of Section 311 in Belarus, Burma, Latvia, Macau, Nauru, Syria, Turkish Republic of Northern Cyprus, and Ukraine.

To determine how Treasury assessed the impact of Section 311 restrictions, we spoke with knowledgeable officials from TFFC and FinCEN as well as officials from State and Justice who had been involved in the 311 process. We also met with foreign government officials in Riga, Latvia; Kyiv, Ukraine; and Macau and Hong Kong, China; as well as with representatives of financial institutions in Latvia, Ukraine, and Macau that were impacted by 311 actions. Also, we reviewed documents identified by Treasury through our document collection instrument as being key documents related to the implementation of Section 311 in Belarus, Burma, Latvia, Macau, Nauru, Syria, Turkish Republic of Northern Cyprus, and Ukraine. We also reviewed documentation, including sensitive and classified cable traffic, which State provided for several 311 cases. State and Treasury provided us with a combination of classified and unclassified documents related to the cases.

We conducted this performance audit from September 2007 through September 2008 in accordance with generally accepted government auditing standards. Those standards require that we plan and perform the audit to obtain sufficient, appropriate evidence to provide a reasonable basis for our findings and conclusions based on our audit objectives. We believe that the evidence obtained provides a reasonable basis for our findings and conclusions based on our audit objectives.

Appendix II: Potentially Relevant Factors for Designating a Jurisdiction or Institution as of Primary Money Laundering Concern

The following table lists information the Secretary of the Treasury is required to consider, in addition to any information that the Secretary determines is relevant, when designating a jurisdiction or institution to be of primary money laundering concern under USA PATRIOT Act Section 311.

Table 1: Potentially Relevant Factors to Be Considered When Designating a Jurisdiction or Institution to Be of Primary Money Laundering Concern

Factors to Be Considered When Designating a Jurisdiction	Factors to Be Considered When Designating an Institution
1. Evidence that organized criminal groups, international terrorists, or entities involved in the proliferation of weapons of mass destruction or missiles have transacted business in the jurisdiction.	1. The extent to which such financial institutions, transactions, or types of accounts are used to facilitate or promote money laundering in or through the jurisdiction including any money laundering activity by organized criminal groups, international terrorists or entities involved in the proliferation of weapons of mass destruction or missiles.
2. The extent to which the jurisdiction or financial institutions operating in that jurisdiction offer bank secrecy or special regulatory advantages to non-residents or non-domiciliaries of that jurisdiction.	2. The extent to which such institutions, transactions, or types of accounts are used for legitimate business purposes in the jurisdiction.
3. The substance and quality of the administration of the bank supervisory and counter-money laundering laws of the jurisdiction.	3. The extent to which such action is sufficient to ensure, with respect to transactions involving the jurisdiction and institutions operating in the jurisdiction, than the purposes of this subchapter continue to be fulfilled and to guard against international money laundering and other financial crimes.
4. The relationship between the volume of financial transactions occurring in that jurisdiction and the size of the economy of the jurisdiction.	
5. The extent to which that jurisdiction is characterized as an offshore banking or secrecy haven by credible international organizations or multilateral expert groups.	
6. Whether the United States has a mutual legal assistance treaty with that jurisdiction, and the experience of United States law enforcement officials and regulatory officials in obtaining information about transactions originating in or routed through or to such jurisdiction.	
7. The extent to which that jurisdiction is characterized by high levels of official or institutional corruption.	

Source: USA PATRIOT Act.

Appendix III: Factors to Consider in Selecting Special Measures

The following are the factors the Secretary of the Treasury is required to consider when selecting special measures for jurisdictions, financial institutions, international transactions, or types of accounts of primary money laundering concern under USA PATRIOT Act Section 311.

1. Whether similar action has been or is being taken by other nations or multilateral groups.

2. Whether the imposition of any particular special measure would create a significant competitive disadvantage, including any undue cost or burden associated with compliance for financial institutions organized or licensed in the United States.

3. The extent to which the action or the timing of the action would have a significant adverse systemic impact on the international payment, clearance, and settlement system, or on legitimate business activities involving the particular jurisdiction, institution, class of transactions, or type of account.

4. The effect of the action on United States national security and foreign policy.

Appendix IV: Additional Information on Section 311 Cases

The following table shows the dates for each finding of money laundering concern, proposed rule, and final rule issued in cases to-date where the U.S. government has applied USA PATRIOT Act Section 311.

Table 2: Issuance of Finding of Primary Money Laundering Concern, Proposed Rule, and Final Rule for Section 311 Cases

Section 311 case	Date of finding of primary money laundering concern	Date of notice of proposed rule	Date proposed rule finalized or withdrawn	Time between proposed rule and finalization or withdrawal (months)	Status of rule	Special measure
Country of Ukraine	12/26/02	N/A[a]	N/A[b]	N/A[c]	N/A[d]	1 — 4[e]
Country of Nauru	12/26/02	04/17/03	4/18/08	60	Withdrawn	5
Country of Burma	11/25/03	11/25/03	4/12/04	5	Finalized	5
Asia Wealth Bank (Burma)	11/25/03	11/25/03	4/12/04	5	Finalized	5
Myanmar Mayflower Bank (Burma)	11/25/03	11/25/03	4/12/04	5	Finalized	5
Commercial Bank of Syria (Syria)	5/18/04	05/18/04	3/09/06	22	Finalized	5
First Merchant Bank OSH Ltd[g] (Turkish Republic of Northern Cyprus)	8/24/04	08/24/04	4/10/08	44	Withdrawn	5
Infobank (includes Belmetalnergo) (Belarus)	8/24/04	08/24/04	Incomplete	N/A[i]	Incomplete	5
Multibanka (Latvia)	4/21/05	04/21/05	7/12/06	15	Withdrawn	5
VEF Bank[a] (Latvia)	4/21/05	04/21/05	7/12/06	15	Finalized	5
Banco Delta Asia (Macau)	9/15/05	09/15/05	3/14/07	18	Finalized	5

Source: Treasury.

[a]Treasury did not issue a proposed rule for Ukraine.

[b]Treasury withdrew the finding of primary money laundering concern on April 17, 2003. However, there was no proposed rule issued.

[c]There was no proposed or final rule for Ukraine. However, there was 4 months between the time the finding of primary money laundering concern was issued and withdrawn.

[d]The finding of primary money laundering concern was withdrawn and no proposed rule was issued in this case.

[e]Treasury did not issue special measures for Ukraine. However, the finding of primary money laundering concern stated that Treasury intended to issue a proposed rule with one or more of special measures 1 through 4.

[i]This proposed rule has been open for 49 months as of the date of this report. Treasury officials stated that they are reviewing whether or not to finalize or withdraw this proposed rule.

GAO-08-1058 USA Patriot Act

[9]First Merchant Finance Ltd., First Merchant International Inc., First Merchant Trust Ltd., and FMB Finance Ltd. are subsidiaries of First Merchant Bank OSH Ltd. The subsidiaries of First Merchant Bank OSH were included in the proposed rule.

Appendix V: Comments from the Department of the Treasury

DEPARTMENT OF THE TREASURY
WASHINGTON, D.C.

UNDER SECRETARY

September 22, 2008

Loren Yager, Ph.D.
Director
International Affairs and Trade
United States Government Accountability Office
441 G Street NW
Washington, DC 20548

Dear Dr. Yager:

Thank you for the opportunity to review the draft Government Accountability Office (GAO) report entitled "USA PATRIOT Act: Better Interagency Coordination and Implementing Guidance for Section 311 Could Improve U.S. Anti-Money Laundering Efforts." The report examines the implementation and impact of an important tool at our disposal to protect the U.S. financial system from significant vulnerabilities: Section 311 of the USA PATRIOT Act. As is evident in your report, Treasury has used this authority since its enactment in 2001 to protect the U.S. financial system from a wide range of threats – from money laundering vulnerabilities in foreign jurisdictions in Asia, Eastern Europe and the Middle East to North Korea-related illicit financial activity. The continued improvement of the use of this powerful, but relatively new, authority is a top priority for the Treasury Department. We welcome your review with an eye toward helping us improve the effectiveness of this tool.

Your report has confirmed our own views that the instances in which Section 311 has been applied by the Treasury Department have furthered its purpose of protecting the integrity of the U.S. financial system. We appreciate the report's determination that the Treasury Department process for implementing Section 311 was consistent with the legal requirements of the USA PATRIOT Act and the Administrative Procedure Act (APA), including regarding consultation with other agencies. In the interest of improving the accuracy and completeness of your report, we have submitted under separate cover suggested corrections to address areas of the report that are factually incorrect or otherwise imprecise. I would like to respond to the report's conclusion that more formal guidance and coordination in exercising Section 311 authorities is needed. As explained below in more detail, we believe that the Treasury Department has well-defined working mechanisms in place to implement Section 311. Nonetheless, I am taking the occasion of this report and the recommendations it offers to re-clarify these mechanisms.

The report explains how the exercise of the Section 311 authority has evolved significantly from the time the initial actions were begun, through the establishment of the Office of Terrorism and Financial Intelligence (TFI) in 2004, and the subsequent operational development of TFI. As part of its mission to enhance national security, TFI harnesses all of the Treasury Department's authorities and resources to identify and address threats to the United States and vulnerabilities in the financial system that terrorist and other criminal organizations can exploit.

Although I was not interviewed, given the GAO's concerns about the relationship between TFI's offices on the question of Section 311 implementation and my role as the senior official within TFI, I believe I am best situated to clarify any misconceptions. In my view, our application of Section 311 has not only been, as you concluded, consistent with all legal requirements and extremely effective, but also that there is now a clear understanding within TFI about how to employ this and other tools for specific issues and targets. In practice, TFI successfully combines the expertise and knowledge of its components, as well as other government agencies, to get the fullest picture of potential targets. I chair several meetings each week with the leadership of TFI components, where we examine the information available to us about various threats and explore what authorities should be employed to address them. I have made it a priority to approach this process in an integrated way in which we first try to understand the nature of the vulnerability or threat and then determine what tool or tools we should use. Although Section 311 is a critically important authority that Treasury can apply, there are numerous other actions that we may take to effectively respond to a particular threat or vulnerability. Each TFI office brings unique capabilities and information to the table in this process. Just as one example, our Office of Intelligence and Analysis (OIA) is a critical part of this process through its expert analysis of information from the intelligence community. We also draw upon the expertise of other agencies in this process. On occasion this may mean arranging special briefings from subject matter experts in other departments. In addition, as you recognized, the Office of Terrorist Financing and Financial Crimes (TFFC), co-chairs with the Justice Department an interagency working group to enrich consultations on vulnerabilities in the international financial system associated with particular institutions or jurisdictions.

Once TFI has determined through this process that Section 311 is the appropriate authority to respond to a particular threat or vulnerability, the responsibility for regulatory actions under Section 311 authority is clear. The Secretary has delegated responsibility for administration of the BSA, as amended to include the authority of Section 311, to the Director of the Financial Crimes Enforcement Network (FinCEN), pursuant to Treasury Order 180-01 of September 26, 2002. This responsibility includes the drafting of a finding of primary money laundering concern, the drafting of a notice of proposed rulemaking (NPRM) to impose special measures, the administration and review of the NPRM public notice-and-comment period and evaluation of comments received, and, as appropriate on the basis of the administrative record, finalization of a rule or in some cases withdrawal of the proposed rulemaking. Other regulatory responsibilities of FinCEN related to Section 311 rulemaking but not addressed in the report include ensuring compliance of U.S. financial institutions with the statutory and regulatory requirements, and consideration of enforcement actions in the event of failures to comply. All of the foregoing are consistent with FinCEN's broader exercise of its regulatory authorities for the administration of the BSA, to make the U.S. financial industry vigilant and hostile to abuse by criminals, terrorist financiers and other illicit actors. In carrying out its regulatory responsibilities, FinCEN collaborates with and relies upon the expertise of its sister offices within TFI.

While the report places great focus on the finalization of Section 311 rulemakings, it is important to keep in mind that the rulemaking action is not an end in itself. The most successful exercise of Section 311 would be where the underlying threat is eliminated, making the final regulatory action itself unnecessary. It is often the case that a money laundering concern derives at least in part from deficiencies in the laws of a foreign jurisdiction. Your report makes clear that individual Section 311 actions we have taken have helped prompt other countries to address and remedy certain deficiencies we identified. In that sense, effective implementation of our strategy to address a particular vulnerability often goes well beyond the regulatory process. Indeed, complementary to, yet distinct from, a Section 311 action, TFI, and TFFC in particular, will often develop a multi-faceted strategy (sometimes involving coordinated action with other agencies and even other governments) to address the identified deficiencies. Examples, either alone or in combination, might include educating the responsible government on the risks and vulnerabilities, offering technical assistance, and providing support or applying political pressure on the regime to improve the legal framework. Even where the jurisdiction recognizes such deficiencies, addressing them appropriately can be expected to take time.

It is important to keep in mind that dynamic when one considers the time period that can elapse between the issuance of a proposed rule under Section 311 and the finalization (or withdrawal) of that proposed rule. As your report explained, there is no legal requirement under Section 311, the APA, or otherwise in the context of most Government rulemakings generally, to finalize proposed rules within a specific time period. To attempt to establish a formulaic approach would not further the purpose of Section 311. A final Section 311 rule is not meant to be a retroactive punitive measure, but instead a proactive measure to protect against risks. We will thus continue to take into account in considering whether and when to finalize a rule, the extent to which we see good faith progress towards mitigating underlying risks, under the unique circumstances of each case.

Finally, I would like to address the report's observations on consultation with other agencies for Section 311 actions. Most, if not all, Section 311 actions have been the result of months of interagency coordination. I can personally attest to the fact that this consultation has sometimes involved coordination at the highest levels of the relevant agencies. While we do not dispute that some individuals in other agencies might have had varying degrees of involvement across the range of Section 311 cases, we do not agree that the Treasury Department's processes for consultation of Section 311 actions hindered any agency's ability to provide meaningful input to those actions. Treasury has not only consistently sought and received valuable input from other agencies, we have responded to it. In some instances, we have delayed proposed Section 311 actions, sometimes for months, due to the concerns of other agencies. In other cases, we have determined, based on the input of other agencies, that another course of action would be more appropriate than using Section 311. As the report notes, we have met in each case all statutory requirements for the use of this authority, including requirements for consultation with other agencies on proposed Section 311 actions. We also have consistently sought input from other agencies earlier, and more often, than we are required to do so, believing that input from a wide spectrum of experts can often increase the chance of success of a Section 311 action.

For the foregoing reasons, we believe that some of the report's conclusions on these issues may have drawn in significant part from actions begun years ago that do not accurately reflect the coordination and implementation of Section 311 within TFI today. Although I believe this is a matter of agreement among all of TFI's leadership, I have reconfirmed with TFI's component offices the importance of continuing to operate in this manner as we go forward and will ensure that these mechanisms are re-clarified in response to this report and its recommendation.

Thank you for your efforts on this important issue, and should you have any additional questions, please do not hesitate to contact me or my staff.

Sincerely,

Stuart A. Levey
Under Secretary
Office of Terrorism and
Financial Intelligence

Appendix VI: GAO Contact and Staff Acknowledgments

GAO Contact	Loren Yager at (202) 512-4347 or yagerl@gao.gov.
Staff Acknowledgments	Anthony P. Moran, Assistant Director; Jeffrey D. Phillips; Lucia DeMaio; Karen A. Deans; Etana Finkler; Mary E. Moutsos; Mark C. Speight; and David S. Dornish made key contributions to this report.

GAO's Mission	The Government Accountability Office, the audit, evaluation, and investigative arm of Congress, exists to support Congress in meeting its constitutional responsibilities and to help improve the performance and accountability of the federal government for the American people. GAO examines the use of public funds; evaluates federal programs and policies; and provides analyses, recommendations, and other assistance to help Congress make informed oversight, policy, and funding decisions. GAO's commitment to good government is reflected in its core values of accountability, integrity, and reliability.
Obtaining Copies of GAO Reports and Testimony	The fastest and easiest way to obtain copies of GAO documents at no cost is through GAO's Web site (www.gao.gov). Each weekday, GAO posts newly released reports, testimony, and correspondence on its Web site. To have GAO e-mail you a list of newly posted products every afternoon, go to www.gao.gov and select "E-mail Updates."
Order by Mail or Phone	The first copy of each printed report is free. Additional copies are $2 each. A check or money order should be made out to the Superintendent of Documents. GAO also accepts VISA and Mastercard. Orders for 100 or more copies mailed to a single address are discounted 25 percent. Orders should be sent to: U.S. Government Accountability Office 441 G Street NW, Room LM Washington, DC 20548 To order by Phone: Voice: (202) 512-6000 TDD: (202) 512-2537 Fax: (202) 512-6061
To Report Fraud, Waste, and Abuse in Federal Programs	Contact: Web site: www.gao.gov/fraudnet/fraudnet.htm E-mail: fraudnet@gao.gov Automated answering system: (800) 424-5454 or (202) 512-7470
Congressional Relations	Ralph Dawn, Managing Director, dawnr@gao.gov, (202) 512-4400 U.S. Government Accountability Office, 441 G Street NW, Room 7125 Washington, DC 20548
Public Affairs	Chuck Young, Managing Director, youngc1@gao.gov, (202) 512-4800 U.S. Government Accountability Office, 441 G Street NW, Room 7149 Washington, DC 20548

Lightning Source UK Ltd.
Milton Keynes UK
UKHW030650260719
346866UK00005B/314/P

9 781289 046538